Mindfulness Meditation

Techniques for Self-Healing, Stress Relief, Deep Sleep and Spiritual Cleansing

Written By

Guided Meditation Therapy

© Copyright 2019 - Guided Meditation Therapy

All rights reserved.

The content contained within this book may not be reproduced, duplicated or transmitted without direct written permission from the author or the publisher.

Under no circumstances will any blame or legal responsibility be held against the publisher, or author, for any damages, reparation, or monetary loss due to the information contained within this book, either directly or indirectly.

Legal Notice:

This book is copyright protected. It is only for personal use. You cannot amend, distribute, sell, use, quote or paraphrase any part, or the content within this book, without the consent of the author or publisher.

Disclaimer Notice:

Please note the information contained within this document is for educational and entertainment purposes only. All effort has been executed to present accurate, up to date, reliable, complete information. No warranties of any kind are declared or implied. Readers acknowledge that the author is not engaging in the rendering of legal, financial, medical or professional advice. The content within this book has been derived from various sources. Please consult a licensed professional before attempting any techniques outlined in this book.

By reading this document, the reader agrees that under no circumstances is the author responsible for any losses, direct or indirect, that are incurred as a result of the use of information contained within this document, including, but not limited to, errors, omissions, or inaccuracies.

Table of Contents

INTRODUCTION 5

CHAPTER 1 – MEDITATION FOR DEEP SLEEP 8

CHAPTER 2 – SELF-HEALING MEDITATION . 19

CHAPTER 3 – MEDITATION FOR STRESS RELIEF 40

CHAPTER 4 – MEDITATION FOR SPIRITUAL CLEANSING 59

CONCLUSION 70

Introduction

Meditation is a free and easy way for you to start to heal yourself. We all have very unique individual minds and bodies. We have to treat them with as much care and respect as possible in order to get the things that we want from this life.

You can start to use these healing practices in order to find better clarity in your mind, body, and soul overall. Oftentimes, we find it hard to sleep because we are so anxious. Thoughts of regrets, and fear over the future can keep us up at night. We all want to be able to get that deep sleep we need and deserve. You can start to relax through meditative practices. Throughout this book, we have provided you with four meditations that will cure any mental ailments that keep you from getting a restful sleep or enjoying a moment of peaceful relaxation.

What you will need for these meditations are a dedicated meditation spot, as well as an open mind. Your meditation spot can simply be your bed, your living room couch, or a nice cozy spot in the backyard. It will be to your benefit to have the same meditation spot throughout all these because the more that you return to the spot, the easier it will be for your mind to snap into that mentality.

Make sure wherever you choose, it is free and clear from distractions. This will include any TV, computer, or other screen. This could be your phone, a tablet, or something else that keeps you from being able to give your full attention to yourself. Ensure that nobody else is around who might be talking or distracting you. You can do these meditations with other people so long as they are participating as well and are not going to be a source of distraction.

Mindfulness Meditation

Make sure that you do not do these meditations while you're driving or operating any sort of vehicle.

If you do, then you might end up falling asleep, and that can be rather dangerous. And be sure wherever you are for these meditations, you give yourself the chance to be able to fall asleep if that should happen. Keep an open mind and let yourself heal.

Chapter 1 – Meditation for Deep Sleep

This first meditation is going to be one that will help you sleep. Oftentimes, we can't get the right sleep because we are stuck thinking about past regrets and fear over what might happen in the future. This meditation is one that is going to take you on a calm and peaceful journey through your mind in order to work through some of your issues so that you can get the best sleep possible. This is one that will be best done when you are about to fall asleep.

Mindfulness Sleep Meditation

Make sure you are in a relaxed place with no distractions around you. Ensure that your back is comfortable, your legs are out, and your arms are hanging loose at your sides or in a comfortable position. Now it is time to relax so that you can get into a deep sleep. You are committed to living a healthy lifestyle for a better sleep, you are prepared. Now, get ready to be as relaxed as possible.

Close your eyes. There is nothing around you. You feel empty, lifeless, and free from all stress. You are simply a body ready to fall asleep.

You have committed yourself all day to living healthier so that you can get a better sleep tonight. You're not just doing this now because you're tired, you're going to be doing this every single night so that you feel better when you wake up. When you are done sleeping, you will feel like a brand new, refreshed and energized person. There's nothing around you that is going to make you feel tired anymore. It is now time to start to focus on your breathing. Notice as your breath comes in and leaves your body. Gently, delicately, and easily.

Your body is gentle now. It is releasing all the hormones needed to make you as sleepy as possible. You are going to drift further and further away into a deep place where you can start to dream. You're going to be completely relaxed, getting as much energy as needed so you can conquer anything that comes your way the next day. You are dedicated to this sleep. Nothing else matters. Everything is passing by you just as gently as you are falling asleep.

Mindfulness Meditation

Each thought that you have is one that gently comes into your mind, but then you push it out just as easily. Nothing around you is scary. Nothing is causing you worry. There's nothing that needs to be focused on right now, other than falling asleep. All of your distractions are gone.

Things that you went through today don't matter anymore. You are not afraid of anything that's going to happen tomorrow. Each day is a new day, and you're going to go for it as energized as possible.

You are mindful now. You were mindful of all of the things that keep you awake; you don't have your phone next to you anymore. It is far away enough so that it will not cause any more distractions. You've been eating the right diet because you know that too much sugar or caffeine is going to keep you up at night. You are mindful of all of these small habits so that you can have a better and deeper sleep at night. You are mindful now of your body. You can feel as the tension releases itself from you into the mattress.

That is why mattresses and pillows are so soft. They help to absorb all of the hard things that we have had to deal with throughout the day. You are becoming more and more relaxed. The air is coming into your body and leaving so slowly. You are very mindful of this. Let's now practice mindful breathing. Notice the air as it enters your body.

Let it come out slowly through your mouth. Breathe in through your nose and out through your mouth. Breathe in. Breathe out. Breathe in, breathe out. Now it is time to start to count your breathing. Counting will make it easier for your breath to come in and out, in and out. Breathe in through your nose now for one, two, three, four, and five.

Mindfulness Meditation

Breathe out for six, seven, eight, nine, and ten.

You are now more relaxed than you were before. You are feeling nothing but gentle delicate air pass in and out through your body. You are one with your surroundings. You are connected to your bed. You are connected to a softer mindset. You are aware of all of the things that make it hard for you to go to sleep. You are very mindful of the situations which cause stress. You are not letting these moments disturb your sleep now. The only thing that matters is that you are focused on sleep. Drifting away is the task that you need to complete in the moment. Making sure that you get a deep sleep is the only thing that you will have to concern yourself with for the next few hours.

You are now more tired than you were before. Your eyes are heavy but not causing pain. You simply cannot keep them open anymore.

You feel yourself sink deeper and deeper into the delicate bed.

You are surrounded by pillows and blankets, all which keep you comfortable and safe. Nothing can hurt you now. Nothing will scare you. You are protected and you are calm. Breathe in again for one, two, three, four, five, and out for six, seven, eight, nine, and ten.

You are now floating. You are in space with nothing around you. All you can see is black. There are some bright stars that dot the sky around you but other than that you are simply floating. You feel nothing at all whatsoever. You are above the earth drifting through space, nothing pulling on you in any way. There is no one that is going to be nagging you. Nobody is there to ask questions. You are completely alone and free and safe. You can't reach out and touch anything. You are simply floating in the air. There is no gravity that keeps you attached to the ground. There is no room that you are in. There is no surface for you to sit. There is no floor for you to stand, there is no wall to keep you confined. None of this scare you. This is exactly what you need, you are in the only place that you need to be in this moment. You are directly in the spot that is going to put you deeper and deeper into sleep.

You feel how every single part of your body is drifting gently. Nothing's weighing you down. You are nothing but a person who is becoming more and more relaxed.

There is no ship taking you through space. There is no surface that you are lying on. You are just you. You are peace. You are calm. You embody everything important about sleep.

Guided Meditation Therapy

You look around and all you see are the stars. There is nothing else that is keeping you distracted at this moment. You are only focused on keeping your eyes closed and drifting further and further away.

You don't notice how your body is moving. You don't notice what position it is in; that does not matter. The only thing that matters now is that we rest our mind. Our minds work so hard throughout the entire day to keep us focused. Our minds are constantly working harder than any other organ that we have in our body. It is time now to pay it back by giving it this deep sleep. You are taking care of your body. You are giving it everything that it needs to properly sleep.

Breathe in for one, two, three, four, five, six, seven, eight, nine, and ten. Breathe out for ten, nine, eight, seven, six, five, four, three, two, and one.

Mindfulness Meditation

There is nothing. You are at peace, you are asleep. You are calm. You are collected. If you still cannot sleep, you can count the stars.

You see so many stars in the sky, and all that matters is that you are focusing on them. Admire their beauty. Look at how they shine and think of nothing else. Be mindful of your surroundings. The only surroundings you have now are the stars. The more mindful you are, the easier it is for you to drift asleep. Each time a scary thought comes into your head, simply look at the stars. Each time you get worried about what happened today, look at the stars. Every moment that you fear will happen tomorrow you ignore and instead, look at the stars. You are reminded of all that surrounds you. When you look to the sky you can remember that your problems aren't so bad after all. You are strong and mighty, yet your problems are miniscule compared to the vast sky above you.

Notice the stars that are bigger than others. Some shine brighter than the ones next to them. Some seem closer and further away, but none of this matter. All that matters are that you notice them and that you count them.

Continue to count them over and over again until you fall asleep. You are now drifting away deeper and deeper, heavier and heavier. When we count to one, you will be completely asleep. Continue to breathe in through your nose and out through your mouth. Breathe in good energy and breathe out everything that might be keeping you awake. Be mindful of your surroundings, only noticing the stars and everything else drifting away. Breathe in. Breathe out. Breathe in. Breathe out.

Breathe in for ten, nine, eight, seven, six, and out for five, four, three, two, one.

Chapter 2 – Self-Healing Meditation

This meditation is one that is going to help you start the healing process. We often look for outside sources to heal ourselves in order to get through some of life's greatest challenges. This meditation is one that is going to remind you that you are capable of healing yourself on your own. You don't have anything to be afraid of and you can work through your anxiety with your own mind. Let yourself heal in this moment and be open to the idea of spiritual cleansing.

Meditation for Self-Healing

It is time for you to start to heal. It doesn't matter how big your scars are, or how long they've been around; your mental wounds are finally coming to an end and it's time to fully heal from them. You have all the power within you already to start this healing process. You want to be able to relax. You need to feel calm and at peace so that you can get some sleep. You want to be able to drift away easily without thinking of everything that keeps you awake at night.

It is time for you to heal yourself. This all starts with our breathing. Everything that comes to you and life can be dealt with through breathing. It is not the answer. It is not the exact solution. It is not a remedy, but it will help you through every other process. The first thing you will always want to do is just breathe. Make sure now that you are in a relaxed place. You might drift asleep and that is perfectly fine. This is all about healing and sleep is important in the healing process.

Start to feel the air as you breathe in. Let it fall out of your mouth delicately and gently.

Mindfulness Meditation

Breathe in now for one, two, three, four, five. And out for six, seven, eight, nine, and ten. One more time for one, two, three, four, five. And out for six, seven, eight, nine, and ten. You are at peace with yourself. You are completely calm and relaxed. There is not an ounce of tension that is left anywhere in your body. You are starting to think about forgiveness. You are understanding what forgiveness means to you. It does not just mean forgetting everything that happened. It doesn't have to mean being okay with somebody who hurt you. Forgiveness is for you. The only reason you will ever forgive is for your own healing process. You are starting to feel more and more at peace with yourself as you think about forgiveness. You are letting go of every emotion that you had, at the time that you were hurt. You are healing yourself through this process. You might be forgiving somebody that is close to you. You might be forgiving yourself. You could be forgiving somebody that you never even met.

Start this forgiving process now. There are no excuses for what has happened. If we don't let go of these emotions, they will only hurt us in the end. You can't heal if you continue to feel hurt over and over again.

You do not have to accept the other person's apology. You do not have to listen to anybody who says they are sorry if you do not want to. You are simply forgiving now to move on. You have a bright future and you have so much to look forward to. You need to get some sleep right now and this is all going to be achieved through forgiveness.

You let go of your past and are no longer chained down by it. Instead, you are letting it thrive so that your future can be bigger and brighter than ever before. Forgiveness is helping you relax. You can start to feel as the tension leaves your body. You are already feeling better about yourself. As you start to forgive, you will fall into a deeper sleep more easily. It is more natural for you to let go of the things that are keeping you chained to your past. In order to fall asleep, it is time to forgive.

You feel yourself getting lighter and lighter and lighter. You are now accepting of the situation you were once in, or of the person that hurt you.

You are protected. You aren't going to let anyone hurt you anymore. You were not in control of the hurt from the past. Someone took something from you, and now you can heal in order to move on. You now know exactly what to do. You are in control. You are in charge of the future that awaits.

You do not have anything to fear in this moment.

You are perfectly fine and capable of everything that comes your way. You are strong and powerful. The strength is what you are going to use to help get you through the forgiving process. The strength is what will give you courage. You will be able to walk through any scary path that might lay ahead. What happened to you in the past is not something that you need to attach yourself to now.

What you might have experienced previously can be separated from now. The only thing that you need to worry about is healing.

You are doing this yourself. You are strong. You are courageous. You are brave. You are letting go of the emotions that have kept you trapped in the same mentality you experienced when you first endured the trauma. You can feel these emotions leaving you now. You will not forget what happened. But you can forget the feelings. You don't

Mindfulness Meditation

have to let those feelings replace the emotions that you have now. You are allowed to be happy. You are allowed to be excited. It is okay for you to have fun. It is okay for you to relax. You need to relax. You need to be at peace. You need to feel acceptance.

This is all going to help you heal. You are healing yourself by relaxing now. You are letting go of everything that has happened to you. You are not tied down by the feelings that you've had. Breathing is going to help you get through this process. Breathing is incredibly important to help you be more at peace with yourself. Healing can only happen when we are ready for it. You need to be relaxed and calm to let these emotions come into your life. Breathe in for one, two, three, four, five, six, seven, eight, nine, and ten. Breathe out for ten, nine, eight, seven, six, five, four, three, two, one.

And again, breathe in for one, two, three, four, five, six, seven, eight, nine, and ten. Breathe out for ten, nine, eight, seven, six, five, four, three, two, and one.

As you breathe in, imagine that you're breathing in a cool color, like blue or purple. You breathe this in and let it fill your entire body. As you breathe out, you see all the negative emotions and feelings leave you. Red and orange come out as you exhale. You breathe in good feelings, forgiveness, and peace. You breathe out hate, anger, and resentment. You breathe in cool, calm, and serenity. You breathe out every emotion that has kept you trapped in the same mentality that you've endured for so long. Notice how much better you feel as you breathe in this love and peace. As you let go of all those harsh emotions, you feel lighter and freer. You are not afraid of the things that happened to you. You do not fear them happening again. You are strong enough to get through them. You can heal yourself through this process. Continue to breathe in and feel yourself healing as you allow cool air to enter your body.

Feel how easier it is to heal as you exhale all of the hate and red that has been enclosed in you for so long. The bluer you breathe in, the better you feel. Notice how your body expands as you start to breathe in. You're filling yourself. You're stuffing your body with good energy. You feel this cool air spread to every last part of your body. You feel it through your legs, all the way down to your toes. You're wrapped up in this calm blue peace. You feel it radiate through your back and down to the tips of your fingers. It spreads through your head, your veins, your blood, your muscles, your bones. This cool blue is everywhere in your body.

The bluer, the easier it is to let go of the red. You continue to allow more and more to come into your life. Making everything else disappear. You are breathing in peace like medicine.

You breathe in and out, in and out.

You breathe in happiness; you breathe out anger. You are not angry about what happened to you now. You could be angry if you wanted to, but that is not going to help you heal.

The only thing that you need to focus on now is being happy yourself, you're breathing out that anger, and it's not something that's going to control you anymore. Before the anger pumped red through your body. It took over and made you a different person. You are taking back your life.

You are not letting this anger define you and your thoughts anymore.

Mindfulness Meditation

You are separating yourself from the deep anger that you used to feel. You breathe in peace; you breathe out fear.

You are not afraid of reliving the past. You do not have to play the scenarios, over and over again.

You are giving yourself the best chance possible to heal now. You breathe in peace, you breathe out anger and hate, you breathe in love. You have love for yourself, you love yourself for being so strong and getting through this. You are so thankful that you have the body that you do.

You are kind to yourself now. You are not someone who needs to be afraid of being yourself. You are feeling strong and encouraged. You have the ability to motivate yourself. You have everything that you could ever need to live a happy and successful life. You are sure about who you are. You might not have it all figured out, but you are confident with who you are. You are loving to yourself because of this. You are able to be compassionate and show yourself empathy when you need it. You do not punish yourself anymore. You are not interested in torturing your own soul. You look past any mistakes you might have made and are only focused on bringing good into your life at this very moment.

You love the person that you have become. You are so proud of your own personal accomplishments. You are very thankful for the body and the life that you have been given.

You have so much love for yourself that you can share that love with other people. You love others and you let them in.

You breathe in peace and love, and you breathe out hate. This hate is directed at yourself. This hate is directed at people who hurt you. You hate yourself because it's easy to blame yourself for what happened to you. This is not what you need to do anymore. No longer do we use blame. Rather than blaming, you now forgive. You don't look for the "why" anymore. You only focus on forgiving. You aren't trying to cast shame onto anyone. You are only interested in healing yourself for the better.

Let go of the hate that you have. Breathe in love and breathe out the hate. This is going to help you heal. When you keep using that hate it spreads red through your body. Calm it down with blue. Feel yourself getting better and better. Feel yourself getting stronger and stronger. You are incredibly brave and nobody, even yourself, can tell you otherwise.

Start to notice now more than ever, how easy it is for you to heal yourself.

It of course has not been easy the entire time, but now you know exactly what needs to get done to feel better. You feel yourself getting better and better, stronger and stronger. You are not going back to the person that you were before the hate. There will be a scar there. The scar is not ugly.

It is not something you need to hide or be afraid of. The scar is now part of who you are. It is going to leave an impression in the way that you think, act, and feel. The things that you went through made you the person that you are now, and that is incredibly beautiful. You are very proud of what this has done for you. You're not proud of what happened to you, but you are proud of the way that you have been able to become a stronger person because of it. You're not letting this take over who you are.

You're not letting it push you back down into a place where you are afraid and too scared to come out of. You are using this opportunity to be a better and stronger person than you ever could have imagined. You are not going back to who you were before this. You wouldn't want to anyway. You knew less than you do now. You are smart and brave, and strong and powerful. You are capable of anything and there's nothing that's going to get in the way from getting the things that you want. You know exactly what you need to do and you are more at peace with yourself now than you ever have been. You continue to feel yourself breathing in the blue, the good, the happy. You breathe out the anger, the hate, and the resentment. You let go of those nasty feelings. It doesn't make you feel good to be so angry. There's no joy coming in from being so scared all the time.

You can't help these feelings in every circumstance, and you are not a bad person for still having these. You know that you simply need to focus on breathing in the good and letting go of the bad instead. You know exactly what you need to do to feel better. You are healing yourself because you are strong, powerful, and amazing. The red was like bacteria that attached itself to every part of your body.

It was a virus, a disease, a cancer that took control of who you are. That's not the case anymore. You're healing your mind and in turn, you're healing your soul. You feel connected to yourself deep down on a different level that you never would have imagined. You are stronger now than anybody could have guessed you would be.

You feel your head becoming lighter. You feel your body becoming brighter. Everything about you is feeling more and more free. You're not attached or glued to the floor anymore. You're not stuck in the same place that made you so scared from the start.

You feel that it's easier to carry your shoulders around. Your head isn't some heavy weight anymore. Now, you are working harmoniously in order to have the best life possible.

You are achieving things that you never thought you could. You radiate happiness; you radiate healing.

You are at peace and it shows. You have a glow around you that makes everybody that comes into contact with you, feel better. You don't have to think of the constant thoughts about what happened to you, or what other people did to you anymore. You're not making yourself feel guilty for anything that you might have put yourself through. You're forgiving of everything that's ever happened to you, and nobody else is going to make you feel bad ever again. You know exactly how to heal yourself. You know how to build yourself up. You know how to talk yourself through the most challenging moments. You know everything that you need to make sure that you can get through any pain again, that is similar to the experiences that you already went through.

Nobody is going to hurt you anymore. Nothing is going to harm you. You are strong, you are brave, you are powerful.

Your stomach feels better. You don't have a pit in there anymore like a black hole that sucked in your soul.

You feel so brave and free, disconnected from the things that used to keep you chained up. There is no rope around your wrists. Nothing holding your ankles down. There is nothing metaphorically or physically that is going to keep you in a place where you aren't allowed to heal. You can take care of yourself. You are capable of finding this peace within your body, you have everything that you could have ever wanted to make sure that you aren't feeling those same challenging thoughts. Continue to feel the air come in through your nose and out through your mouth. Count as the blue comes in and count down as the red leaves. Breathe in the good and out the bad.

Breathe in the love and out the hate. Breathe in the happiness and out the anger. Let go of these feelings. Watch as they drift through the air and away from you, never to hurt you again. Even if they do come back, you are stronger now and you can fight them. Even if something terrible does happen now, you know exactly how to guide yourself through it.

You don't need anybody else to heal. You can do this all on your own. You have so much to be proud of. You are so brave; you feel yourself becoming more and more relaxed. You are more at peace now than you ever thought you could have been. You never imagined that you would be able to be so strong and so brave, yet here you are. You are more and more relaxed, the more that you continue to breathe in the blue and out the red.

The red is changing now. As you breathe out, it's becoming softer and softer. It's like a gentle pink. You can still see the hints of what was once there, but no longer is this going to be something that spreads sickness through the air. Now you breathe in blue, happiness, purple, green.

All of these cool colors help relax you.

As you breathe out, it's a soft and gentle pink. It spreads through the air, and through other people. This energy is contagious. It helps not only you but those around you heal also. You have incredible power, and you are capable of anything. Breathe in again for five, four, three, two, one.

Breathe out for one, two, three, four, and five. Continue this over and over. As you continue to drift further and further from your waking life and deeper and deeper into sleep, you can sleep peacefully. Now, you can sleep without any fear. There's nothing around you that you have to be afraid of. You have everything inside of you in order to make it through. You are strong, you are brave, you are free.

Chapter 3 – Meditation for Stress Relief

This meditation is a basic one that will help relieve your stress. It is a visualization meditation, where you will be taken through a small journey. You will be able to come out of this with a light feeling and an airy mind that gives you the clarity needed to get the right things done.

Stress Relieving Meditation

It's time to go on a journey. At the beginning of this journey, you are somebody who is filled with stress. The stress keeps you awake at night to the point where you can't even fall asleep anymore. This is not who you're going to be by the end of the journey.

By the end of the journey, you're going to be incredibly tired. You will be so relaxed, that the only thing that you can do is think about closing your eyes and falling asleep. No longer are you going to allow yourself to be awake all night thinking of terrible things that might pass through your head. Rather than focusing on the bad, we are going to be looking at the good. You are going to be stronger and braver at the end of this. The stress relief is going to help you be as relaxed as possible. You will feel good not only when going to bed, but throughout your entire day.

Pick somewhere now where you can be completely calm and relaxed. You can be lying in bed ready to drift away to sleep, or you can simply be sitting in your backyard enjoying the nature around you. Wherever you are, ensure that you can be completely at peace. Remove all distractions, any noise, or anything else that is going to keep you pulled from this meditation and stuck in the moment that's surrounding you. Start to notice the way that you're breathing. Breathe in for a few moments and then breathe out. Breathe in, breathe out.

Feel the air come in through your nose and let it leave through your mouth. This is a common way to practice breathing so that you can be more relaxed. You don't have to do this just when you want to go to bed. You can do this at any moment when you want to bring calmer and serenity into your life. Close your eyes and make sure all thoughts leave your mind. Anytime a thought passes through your mind, gently push it away as if it were a cloud in the sky. Remember that as you continue to think of thoughts that might flood your mind, simply let them pass, not giving them any attention at all. The only thing you should be focusing on now is being as relaxed as possible.

Mindfulness Meditation

Look in front of you as you close your eyes. Keep your eyes straight forward, and imagine nothing but blackness. Don't drift away into an imagery, or a fantasy. Simply continue to keep your eyes closed. Look ahead of you now into the darkness that is behind your eyelids.

Nothing is in front of you. The only thing that you need to focus on now is being as calm and relaxed as possible. In front of you, you see a little bright light. It is nothing more than the size of a penny. You continue to see it grow and grow.

It gets bigger and bigger, until you see that there is a path in front of you. In your mind, you take a step forward. It is a nature walk. This path is going to take you through the forest.

You are completely at peace, calm, and centered, looking at nothing but what is in front of you. The sidewalk is gray stone, and you take a step forward. You are now completely relaxed. Nothing occupying your mind, other than the sites that you see around you. On your left is a lush green forest. On your right is a large calm and cool body of water. It is a lake, nothing special about it.

It is like many other lakes that you pass. This one in particular is sticking out to you now, because you are more and more relaxed. Now that you have no stress to focus on, you can look ahead of you and see everything that is beautiful about this area. You continue to walk forward, more and more trees emerging each step that you take. On the right, where rocks lines the coast, green leaves stick out through these rocks with large bushes also appearing every once in a while. There are some sticks and other stones lying at the surface of the water with waves splashing against them over and over again.

You continue to walk forward looking at the vast blue on your right. You see a path emerge on the left; you decide to follow it and the sidewalk is now gone. There's nothing but dirt. You take a step forward and you can still see the blue on your right side. You are simply now further and further away from it than you were before. You continue on this path and beneath your feet, you see a log. The log must have fallen recently in a storm. You step over it, ignoring that's even there.

There's nothing in particular about this log that is keeping you down. You simply step over it and continue to move on the path that gets higher and higher and you can see more and more of the blue water next to you. Behind the water is a large mountain covered in lush green. All around you is green, blue, and brown. It is nature, it is the earth, you are connected to it.

You see the blue beneath you. But you continue to step forward on the path. Nothing is getting in your way. You can hear the cicadas, the bees, and other bugs flying around in the woods, but none of this scares you. There's nothing that you have to worry about now. You are simply enjoying all the wonderful sights around you.

You are further and further from the water now elevated several feet above. There's a few more trees and the lush green on your right is getting greater.

Every once in a while, as you keep moving forward, you occasionally notice more branches, trees, and bushes. You notice how nature changes itself without any help. Trees fall but then a new one grows in its place. Flowers bloom. Bees pollinate, and they continue to grow greater and greater. Water is the source of so much of this. Water is where animals and nature connect. Different animals approach the water to drink from it. Birds fly over-top and land in the bushes.

It is a gorgeous site that is keeping you extremely relaxed. You could certainly find something to be afraid of. Maybe the height, the bugs, or even a snake. None of this matters now, however. You only care about being as relaxed as possible. You get to a point where there's a large tree hanging over the trail.

It casts a shadow and gives you a moment to appreciate the darkness; even when the sun is absent this beauty still exists. It even transformed throughout the day as well. Always looking a little bit different.

Throughout all of the green, wild flowers emerge.

It's not like the strict landscaping that you see it in some people's houses. It is nature creating its own beautiful patterns. There are some blue flowers here and some white flowers there.

Sometimes the flowers cross over the path connected only by their color. There are yellow little dots all throughout, some long purple strands, and even a few red flowers. There is no order to this, they simply grow where they had been planted.

Even though it might not have been planned out, they're still so beautiful. Now, a butterfly comes and passes over the path. It continues to fly around you and you appreciate its unique beauty. This used to be something that looked like a little worm, but it is now a beautiful butterfly. You are not afraid of it. You're not afraid of any of these little critters or gorgeous little parts of nature.

You go left a little bit more.

You see another path that takes you deeper into the forest. You're not going to go up to the water anymore. You want to get deeper and deeper into nature. You see birds, leaves, trees, and other gorgeous things above you and swallowing you as if you were becoming part of it yourself. It helps make you completely at peace. There is nothing around you, which scares you in this moment. You are on your own, and that is, OK. You feel completely relaxed and at ease when you are surrounded by greenery. Nothing could ever cause you stress.

When there is so much beauty around you to appreciate, how could you ever have worries over things that are so small? These plants don't have worries. These flowers aren't afraid. You continue, placing one foot in front of the other.

Notice your breath again now. With each step you take in a new breath. Breathe in for one, two, three, four, and five. Breathe out for five, four, three, two, and one.

You are completely at ease. You are entirely relaxed, nothing around you can cause you fear or anxiety. You go deeper and deeper into the forest. There is nothing but trees and wildflowers now. They all stand so tall, pointed towards the sun. The cycle of life is overwhelming. It radiates through your body, and you are reminded of who you truly are. You are not defined by the things that cause you stress. You do not have to worry about what you cannot control. There will always be so many surprises in life, and this does not scare you. It empowers you. There are so many uncertainties that we might run into, but none of this causes you fear, it makes you feel good. It makes you feel strong, it makes you feel brave. You are part of nature, you work with it. You are one with your surroundings.

Breathe in again for five, four, three, two, one, and out for one, two, three, four, and five. Feel as the nature that surrounds you becomes a part of who you are. Each breath that you take is one which fills you with happiness, peace, and serenity. The air you breath sends oxygen all throughout your body, becoming a part of the cycle of your system. You absorb everything around you through the air that you are breathing.

You see nothing around you now but the trees. The water is out of sight, you continue to walk deeper and deeper into the woods. You are entirely at peace, nothing around you that reminds you of what you experienced before is causing you any stress or anxiety now. You are completely and entirely free from the things that used to scare you.

It can be hard to know how to heal ourselves and to reduce our stress when your brain is so stressed out. How could you even possibly manage to think of a way to lift yourself up from this challenging mood? Now, you know, when you are stressed, you can come back to this for those purposes. Each step you take is one dedicated to being more calm. You continue to walk deeper into the woods and ahead of you, you notice a river.

It is a calm stream, but you can still hear the water running. You think about the water that you had just seen, and you realize it must lead to a waterfall.

Maybe one day you'll visit that waterfall. But for now, you choose to step towards the stream and watch as the water passes on the surface of the stream. There are leaves floating towards the waterfall. You can't see the endpoint, but you know where they're going and what their destination is.

You simply watch the leaves pass gently through the stream and away from you.

These leaves can represent your thoughts. Your thoughts can flow gently towards you, and you can choose to stop them. You could choose to stand in front of these leaves and pick them up. If you were submerged yourself in the water, the leaves would stick to you, the same way your beliefs do.

You could change the direction that they move in, but you don't have to do that. You can simply notice the leaves and let them continue on in their journey. Do this with your thoughts as your thoughts trickle in. Just leave them be, let them pass through your mind, and focus your attention on something new. Maybe you'll find that one special leaf that you decide to pick out and choose to keep. That is okay, but you can't do that with every leaf. You have to make it special.

You continue to walk along the stream. Noticing all the different shapes of the little rocks that lay at the bottom.

Every once in a while, you'll see a little fish dart away. Does this fish know where it is? Why does this fish wrongly swim against the current?

Does this fish know what's waiting for it if it follows the current?

What would happen if it did choose to just swim and turn around?

These thoughts simply pass through your mind, but you don't attach an emotion to them. You don't need to feel stressed or scared in this moment, you are perfectly fine. Continue on.

You step further down the stream and you notice the turtle submerging itself into the water. There's a little frog as well hopping around. They enjoy nature, but do they appreciate it the same way you do?

These questions, they don't need answers, but it helps to think about them. It can be a distraction from your stressors. You look up and see a deer. You freeze knowing that if you make any sudden movement, the deer will run away. The deer is not relaxed.

It is always on high alert for anything dangerous that might surround it. The deer does not understand that it doesn't have to live like this. You crouch down letting it know that you are not going to harm it. You look ahead and the deer dips its neck low sticking its tongue out into the cool fresh water. It takes a few sips feeling hydrated and refreshed. You appreciate that this deer is now trusting of you.

It looks back at you before it walks away into the forest. The deer is just like you.

You don't have to be so afraid thinking there is a threat standing across the stream. Sometimes, it could be something that could help you instead.

This fills you with peace. You turn around and decide that it is now time to head back home. You haven't completed the path but you don't have to. It's okay to just enjoy a little bit at a time. Not everything has to be done to completion. You start to walk back, but now you notice all these things so differently. The sun is starting to set, so it's getting darker and darker. More animals are hiding as others emerge. You can hear the sound of crickets as they replace the buzz of cicadas. You hear frogs start to emerge from their daily slumbers to catch any flies or mosquitoes that are going to be out tonight.

What was on one side before is now on the other side as you walk back down the path. You can start to see the water again, the cool blue. There are a few people splashing around and taking a relaxing dip in the distance.

You pay no mind to them, they are having their own fun. You are focused on yourself. You're getting closer and closer now to the beginning of the path, you feel more and more relaxed, you are at peace with yourself and the world in which you live in. There is nothing that scares you. You don't have to be afraid or fearful, nothing's going to harm you. You're more relaxed now than you could ever imagine that you would be. You are leaving this forest, a new person. This walk has changed you. You are now letting go of all the stress and tension that you have been carrying around. There is no need to hold onto stressful thoughts.

You leave all that behind, in nature. It is going to become one with its surroundings. Now, you can see the end of the path, and it is almost night.

Slowly bring yourself back to where you are in the present moment. Feel your breath go in and out. Breathe in for one, two, three, four, and five and out for five, four, three, two, and one. Continue to breathe. Your eyes are still closed and heavy. The forest in front of you is now fading to black. Just like the bright light that emerged earlier, this light is now becoming smaller and smaller.

You are back home again, and you can feel your surroundings. You are connected to them, and one with nature. You are not afraid, fearful, stressed, or angry. You are just you.

As we count down from 20, you will slowly fall into sleep or move on to the next meditation.

Twenty, nineteen, eighteen, seventeen, sixteen, fifteen, fourteen, thirteen, twelve, eleven, ten, nine, eight, seven, six, five, four, three, two, one.

Chapter 4 – Meditation for Spiritual Cleansing

This final meditation is one that is going to teach you how you can go through spiritual cleansing. This is going to be a method that will help cleanse you and your thoughts. We have provided you with the right mindset tools needed for you to heal from anything that might have happened while preparing for greater challenges as well.

Spiritual Cleansing Meditation

We often pay attention to how we can heal our minds or our bodies, but we need to remember to heal our spirit as well. Spiritual cleansing doesn't have to be about some mystical voodoo magic that is unexplained. Your spirit is a part of you; it is who you are. It is the character that you have built. It is what you believe, it is your virtue. It is your dedication and passion.

Your spirit is a part of who you are and we need to figure out how to heal it. We are going to take you through the steps of spiritual cleansing. This is something you can do daily, weekly, or monthly. As long as you are dedicating time to cleansing your spirit, you will notice the many benefits of this meditation practice.

Start first by going to a place where you can completely shut out and relax. Free yourself of all distractions.

Begin by breathing in, for five, four, three, two, one, and out for one, two, three, four, five. Again, breathe in for five, four, three, two, one, and out for one, two, three, four, five.

Mindfulness Meditation

Continue this as we take you through the journey of spiritual healing.

First, we need to learn how to appreciate our bodies.

Our bodies are the spiritual vessels that we interact with throughout the world. Your body helps carry you throughout your day-to-day life. Your body is like a tool that our spirit needs in order to thrive and survive.

Begin to appreciate your body.

Start from the very top of your head and work your way all the way down to the tips of your toes. Breathe in for five, four, three, two, one and out for one, two, three, four, five. Notice now how connected you feel to your body as you start to breathe.

You can feel the air as it fills every last part of your body. The place that needs the air the most is your brain. This is at the very top of your head. Your brain holds together your spirit and your mind.

You spirit is who you are. It is how you think that makes you a unique individual person. It is the way that you are able to love and understand others, which creates a unique character within yourself. Your spirit is somebody strong and passionate. Your spirit helps you find your motivation and your dedication.

Thank yourself. Give gratitude to this incredible brain that we have. Even when it might not think something that we want, or might cause us to say something that we don't even mean, we still have to appreciate all the good that our brain can do for us. Begin to work your way down now to your face. This is how you tell others what your spirit is feeling. You can smile. You can cry. You can laugh. You can show anger, interest, intrigue, or curiosity.

Mindfulness Meditation

Your face is an incredible tool that your spirit uses to share a message. We can use our mouth to talk, our mouth to eat, and our mouth to breathe. This is so powerful, all in one tiny spot on your entire body. Feel this part of you now as you relax further and further. Feel how the air coming into your body fills you with everything needed to feel better. Allow this meditation to be one where you are saying thanks to your body. Appreciate each little vessel that we discuss.

Your eyes are able to see so much. You can pick up on things around you that others might not even see. You're able to use your eyes to discover the things that you love. Your eyes help you see the people that you care about most. They make you a strong person who's able to complete tasks efficiently.

Move down now to your ears. Your ears can help you hear and understand everything that's around you. You have no problem hearing all that's important. Your ears allow you to hear fun and exciting news. You can hear music and movies that you enjoy and love watching. Your ears are incredibly powerful.

Move down to your shoulders. Your shoulders are what can connect your arms to the rest of your body. These arms are so powerful. They can carry and hold loved ones. They can help you lift things up when needed. You can create with these arms and these hands. Your fingers can touch and they give you greater insight into what things you enjoy. You can make food and other people happy all by using your hands. You can touch somebody's face, and let them know that you're close to them. You can rub their back and make them feel better. You can hold and embrace them so that they don't feel scared or alone.

Breathe in and feel the air travel through these parts of your body. Allow yourself to find a deeper connection to your arms and your hands. Allow yourself to relax these parts of your body.

Move to your chest. Your chest is where your heart beats. The beating of your heart can tell you how you feel. When its rapid and quick, it tells you that you're scared or worried. When it's slow and heavy, it's nice and relaxing. Close to your heart are your lungs. Breathe in again now and feel as your body fills with air.

Breathe in for one, two, three, four, and five, and out for five, four, three, two, and one. Feel this incredible strength as it travels in and out. You are capable of everything, because of your heart, your lungs, and your brain. You can accomplish anything that you need to feel better in this life. Move down now to your stomach. Your stomach can tell you so much. It gives you an intuition. You have a gut feeling that can make it easier for you to decide what might be good for you and what might not be in any given situation. This is your power. It's what makes you capable of anything in this world. You are incredibly strong. You have all it takes to heal your spirit.

Now let's remind ourselves of how this body can connect us to the earth. The earth is like our mother; it is where we are born. It is where everything that we have ever experienced has occurred. Unless you are an astronaut, you have only ever been on this earth. You can put your feet in the dirt or sand to feel more connected. You can be surrounded by plants and trees that fill you with healthy air. Your friends and family that can make you feel better about yourself or a situation. You can be engulfed with love and passion and happiness. All of these things are going to be incredibly important for you.

Mindfulness Meditation

Not only are you connected to the earth, but you are also connected to your body. Look at all the other animals that surround you. They have bodies too. All bodies are different. Some are big, some are small, some are tall, some are short. Some are healthy, some aren't.

Your body is yours, and it is the only one that you will ever have. We don't know what happens in this next life and if we get a new body or not. Maybe our body transforms or maybe it just goes away forever, none of this matters now.

Heal yourself, feel your spirit become cleaner, knowing how deeply connected you are to your body. You feel incredibly powerful, safe, and secure. Let go of everything that has happened to you. This is how we can heal our minds. Our minds carry all of our emotional states, they keep around memories that might hurt us, or they make us think darker thoughts that can be challenging to deal with. Your mind is incredibly important as well. We need to clean up this mind. Let all of your thoughts drift away. Think of them like passing raindrops on a car window. They hit the window but then they fall away and dissolve into other little droplets. Let your thoughts heal just like this. You can keep those thoughts around, but transform them and learn how to use them. Pull the good and focus on that rather than getting stuck with the negative ones. When you can heal your mind and your body, you are cleansing your soul. You are dedicated to healing. You make it your focus to be as passionate and calm as possible.

Now you are going to become more and more relaxed. This is how you are going to continue to heal.

Mindfulness Meditation

Spiritual cleansing will always be important for you to feel better. In the end, let your mind drift away, and allow your body to become relaxed and happy. You are clean. You are pure, you are fresh, you are energized, you are rejuvenated. This is all incredibly important and gives us the spiritual healing that we need.

Breathe in for one, two, three, four, and five, and out for five, four, three, two, one. As we count down from twenty, you will either drift off into sleep or move on to a new meditation.

Twenty, nineteen, eighteen, seventeen, sixteen, fifteen, fourteen, thirteen, twelve, eleven, ten, nine, eight, seven, six, five, four, three, two, one.

Conclusion

Repeat these meditations as needed. The more that you practice them, the easier it will be to find valuable healing benefits within them. As with all meditations, ensure that you never do them while operating a vehicle as you could fall asleep. Also, ensure that you find a quiet space free of any distractions.

After you have practiced meditation a few times, you could try to do it somewhere else, such as on an airplane or traveling when you are not the one who is in charge of moving the vehicle.

It could help you relax in the right settings, but you have to get used to what you might do after these meditative practices. The more that you practice them, the easier it will be for your mind to click into this place when necessary.

Mindfulness Meditation

Check out the other meditation books in the series to find something valuable based on your specific needs. Keep an open mind and allow healing into your life whenever possible.

www.ingramcontent.com/pod-product-compliance
Lightning Source LLC
Chambersburg PA
CBHW060412080526
44583CB00012B/538